UNDERSTANDING
COMMUNION

Also by Selwyn Hughes in this series

Understanding Guidance
Understanding the Presence of God

UNDERSTANDING
COMMUNION

by

Selwyn Hughes

CWR

CWR, Waverley Abbey House,
Waverley Lane, Farnham, Surrey GU9 8EP

NATIONAL DISTRIBUTORS
Australia: Christian Marketing Pty Ltd., PO Box 154,
North Geelong, Victoria 3215.
Tel: (052) 786100
Canada: Christian Marketing Canada Ltd.,
PO Box 7000, Niagara on the Lake, Ontario LOS 1TO.
Tel: 416 641 0631
Republic of Ireland: Scripture Union
Book & Music Centre,
40 Talbot St., Dublin 1
Tel: 363764
Malaysia: Salvation Book Centre, (M) Sdn. Bhd.,
23 Jalan SS2/64, 47300 Petaling Jaya, Selangor
New Zealand: CWR (NZ), PO Box 4108,
Mount Maunganui 3030.
Tel: (075) 757412
Singapore: Alby Commercial Enterprises Pte Ltd.,
Garden Hotel, 14 Balmoral Road, Singapore 1025
Southern Africa: CWR (Southern Africa), PO Box 43,
Kenilworth 7745, South Africa.
Tel: (021) 7612560

© CWR 1991
Text originally published 1988, revised and first printed
in this format 1991

Typeset by J&L Composition Ltd, Filey, North Yorkshire

Printed in Great Britain by BPCC Hazell Books,
Aylesbury, Bucks.

ISBN 1–85345–046–4

Bible quotations are taken from the Holy Bible, New
International Version, © 1973, 1978, 1984, International
Bible Society

Contents

INTRODUCTION

"And Jesus took bread, gave thanks and broke it, and gave it to them saying, 'This is my body given for you; do this in remembrance of me.' In the same way, after the supper he took the cup, saying, 'This cup is the new covenant in my blood, which is poured out for you.'" (Luke 22:19 & 20).

Almost every Christian participates from time to time in a service of Communion. We call the service different things: 'the Sacrament', 'Holy Communion', 'the Lord's Supper', 'the Lord's Table', 'the Breaking of Bread', or 'the Eucharist'. How ever, how many of us, I wonder, understand the deep significance that lies behind the simple act of eating the bread and drinking the wine? Over the years I have questioned believers of all denominations as to how they perceive the act of "Holy Communion" and, generally speaking, I have been astonished at the low level of spiritual understanding. Why is it that an event which was intended by our Lord to be a source of continuous spiritual enrichment is, for many, nothing more than a ritual? *I am convinced myself that one of the most urgent needs of the contemporary Christian Church is to return to the true meaning of the Communion.*

If we fail to understand what is involved in this great commemorative act then our meeting together around the Lord's Table will have little spiritual impact on our lives – individually or corporately. Those who see it as nothing more than a sentimental forget-me-not service will, as a result, be spiritually poorer. Those who see it for what it is – a service of deep spiritual significance – will be continually enriched, enlightened and satisfied. So we need to ask ourselves this searching question: have we allowed our familiarity with the act of 'Holy Communion' to breed within us a sense of complacency? Many ministers, myself included, would argue that to a large extent we have.

Roy Peacock in his little book, *This Do Ye*, says: "To many, the Communion service has taken on the form of an abstract set of actions performed, as one would watch a stage play, with interested or perhaps uninterested detachment. No longer do we hear the voice of Jesus saying: 'Do this in remembrance of me.' No more is there the revelation that amazes us, challenges us and changes us, for our ears have waxed heavy and our eyes have been shut by a complacency of satisfaction." He is generalising, of course, but even if the charge of complacency does not apply to us, every one of us cannot help but benefit from the attempt to comprehend more deeply the meaning of the Communion.

We meet around many tables during the course of our lives, but no table is more sacred and meaningful than the one on which we place the simple emblems of bread and wine, and celebrate our Lord's vicarious death and victorious resurrection. Remember: the Communion service is not a matter of inclination – it is a matter of command. Our Lord says: "*Do this* – in remembrance of me." If we are not willing to do this in remembrance of Him, then it is questionable whether we can do anything in remembrance of Him.

Prayer:

My Father and my God, as I begin this study of Communion, help me to see its meaning and its purpose more clearly than I ever have before. In Christ's Name, I pray. Amen.

CHAPTER 1

THE
FIRST
COMMUNION

"While they were eating, Jesus took bread, broke it, and gave it to his disciples . . ." (Matthew 26:26)

If the Christian Church is greatly in need of returning to the true meaning of the Communion, how do we go about this supremely important task? There is a law of Biblical interpretation known as "the law of first occurrence" which states that whenever you wish to understand a truth of Scripture, you should examine in detail the first occasion when that truth is mentioned.

If we are to understand the deep meaning that lies in the commemorative act of Holy Communion, then our first task must be to focus our attention on the very first Communion service that was ever conducted in history – the one held by our Lord that fateful night in the Upper Room. When a jeweller wants to show off a diamond to its best advantage, he puts it on a background of black velvet. There, as the light strikes it, the diamond seems to catch fire, whereupon its beauty and brilliance is greatly magnified and its value made more apparent.

The Lord's Supper is like that diamond. It needs to be prised from its traditional setting where, by reason of endless controversy, it borders on becoming lacklustre, and set against the velvet of the blackest night in history – the night before our Lord was crucified.

It is only there, in its original setting, with the light of the Holy Spirit falling upon it, that it yields its true and proper meaning. I repeat: if we do not understand what happened at that very first Communion service, then we will not be able to understand what it means for us now – here in the 20th century.

Passover – the pattern for Communion

Before we begin a detailed examination of the first Communion service in history, which, as you know, was also our Lord's last corporate activity with His disciples, we refer briefly to the event that led to the institution of what we now call "Holy Communion" – namely, the feast of the Passover. More will be said about this later, but the feast of the Passover was the annual celebration of the night when the Angel of Death passed over the land of Egypt and spared the firstborn of the children of Israel (Exodus chapter 12).

There is no evidence that our Lord and His disciples had shared together in the ceremony of the Passover on previous occasions. It is probable that they had done so, but we cannot be certain. We know, however, that the disciples had been with Him on two previous Passover festivals and, on both these occasions, something unexpected and unusual had taken place. On the first occasion, our Lord entered the Temple and, in an act of righteous indignation, proceeded to empty it of the money changers who, He said, had turned His Father's house into "a den of thieves" (John 2:13–16). On the second occasion, He performed the miracle of the feeding of the five thousand (John 6:1–14).

I wonder, did the disciples think to themselves as, once again, the Passover approached: what surprises will the Master have for us on this occasion? Will He once again do the unexpected and the unusual? It is only conjecture, of course, but if this thought did arise in their minds, they could have had no idea that they were about to be witnesses at the most central Passover of all time, and be observers of an event that would change the entire course of history.

At the beginning of the Passover, Jesus issues the disciples with a set of unexpected instructions: "As you enter the city, a man carrying a jar of water will meet you. Follow him to the house that he enters, and say to the owner of the house . . . Where is the guest room, where I may eat the Passover with my disciples? . . . Make preparations there" (Luke 22:10–12). There can be little doubt that the knowledge our Lord had concerning the man and the room was supernatural, but there is another point to be noted here: that is, the complete and utter confidence the disciples had in the word and command of Jesus. No one remonstrated with Him and said: "But, Master, men don't usually carry jars of water – that is normally the task that women perform." Neither did they say: "Lord, what will this man think of us when we attempt to follow him?" The disciples had obviously learned to trust the word of Jesus and to act, without questioning, upon His commands.

This is a lesson every one of us needs to learn. How often things go wrong in our lives because we cavil at our Master's commands. I wonder, am I talking to someone at this very moment who is hesitating or drawing back from something the Lord has shown you that He wants you to do? If so, then let me give you the word that Mary, our Lord's mother, once gave to a group of interested but hesitant people: "Do whatever he tells you" (John 2:5).

The first Passover

If we are to comprehend the real meaning of the Communion, then we must understand what the feast of the Passover was all about, for it was out of that that the first Communion service emerged. During the time of Israel's bondage and slavery in Egypt, God spoke to Pharaoh through Moses and warned him that on a certain day, at the hour of midnight, He was going to pass through the land and strike down every firstborn. There was to be no discrimination between human beings and animals, or between different social classes – every firstborn would die (Exodus chapter 11).

God then devised a plan whereby the firstborn of His own people, the Israelites, would be protected (Exodus chapter 12). Each Israelite was to choose a lamb (a year-old male without defect) and kill it. They were then to take some of the lamb's blood, dip a branch of hyssop in it and sprinkle it on the sides and tops of their front door frames. They were not to go out of the house at all that night. Having shed and sprinkled the blood, they must shelter under it. At midnight, the Angel of Death passed through the land, and, in every house which did not have a blood-sprinkled door, the firstborn died. The God who passed *through* Egypt in judgment passed *over* every blood-marked dwelling place – hence the term, 'Pass-over'.

Mark this and mark it well – if rubies or some other precious stones had gleamed like red flames from every door, it would not have saved the firstborn of the children of Israel. God had decreed that it was by the shedding of blood that they were to be saved. If the Israelites had stumbled here, they would never have made it to this point in history.

On Passover night itself, the Israelites were told to feast on a roasted lamb, with bitter herbs and unleavened bread, and they were to do so with their cloak tucked into their belt, their shoes on their feet, and their staff in their hand, ready to make a quick departure from the land of bondage. The night of the Passover was so important that it marked the beginning of a new year for Israel – "This month is to be the first month of your year" (Exodus 12:2). From that day to this, the Jewish religious new year begins with 'Pesach' – the Hebrew word for 'Passover'. God gave the Israelites an instruction that this feast should be commemorated throughout the generations to come, and families should explain to their children what the whole ceremony meant: "It is the Passover sacrifice to the Lord, who passed over the houses of the Israelites in Egypt and spared our homes when he struck down the Egyptians" (Exodus 12:27).

This celebration was to last seven days and be known also as the feast of Unleavened Bread, during which time the Israelites were to remind themselves that their deliverance from Egypt's bondage had been planned by Jehovah, purchased by blood and implemented by divine power. Being a redeemed people, this meant that they belonged to the Almighty in a special way and were, therefore, to be consecrated to His service, and be an illustration to the world of what redeemed people should be like.

CHAPTER 2

THE
LAST
SUPPER

". . . So they prepared the Passover." (Mark 14:16)

Having seen what the feast of the Passover means and why it was to be annually celebrated, we return now to the details of the last Passover feast which Jesus commemorated with His disciples. Upon finding the room in which the Master planned to celebrate the Passover, the disciples began at once to make the preparations for the feast.

Although every one of the four gospels contains an account of the Last Supper, we are not given any details as to how the feast was prepared and what items were placed on the Passover table. We know, from the instructions given by God in the Old Testament and tradition, that certain items would be laid out on the table. There would have been a supply of bitter herbs – a reminder of the sufferings that their forefathers went through in Egypt. Another item would have been a bowl of salt water to remind them of the tears that were shed during the years of bondage and slavery. A further item would have been grated apple mixed with nuts and made into a paste (called 'charoseth') which would resemble the colour of clay, and thus remind them of the endless amount of bricks that were made in Egypt.

Yet another item would have been the unleavened bread, the absence of yeast symbolising the haste of that unforgettable night, as well as the need to break with the 'leaven' of evil. On the table, too, would have been an egg symbolising new life, candles to remind them of the worship that went on in the Tabernacle, wine to symbolise the shedding of blood, and last but not least – a roasted lamb. All this had a supreme and important purpose – the event must be kept alive in the memory of Israel. Great events ought never to be forgotten.

It seems remarkable, on the surface of it, that a commemorative event should really be necessary. You would have thought that, with such an out-standing event as the deliverance from Egypt, future generations of Israelites would have talked about it not once a year but every day of their lives! Why should they need a visible and concrete reminder of the event in the form of a seven-day feast?

Memorial stones

God gave them this instruction because He knew the terrible tendency of the human heart to forget. It is simply astonishing how easily we can blot out from our minds not only the unpleasant things of the past but the great and important ones as well. It was because of this that God instructed the Israelites, after they had miraculously crossed over the Jordan, to build a monument of stones so that future genera-tions would be prompted to ask: "What do these stones mean?" (Joshua 4:1–7).

One of the most devastating effects of sin is the paralysis it brings to both mind and memory. Dr Martyn Lloyd-Jones said: "We are so dull and stupid as the result of sin, that we might even forget the death of the Son of God for us, if the Lord Himself had not ordained and commanded that we should meet together and take bread and wine. It is the setting up of the stones in Gilgal once more." We suffer so much from the effects of the Fall that we need objective things and tangible reminders – something outside of ourselves – that will lead us to ask: "What do these stones mean?"

There are many reasons that could be given for the benefit that comes from commemorating divine acts and events but perhaps the biggest reason is this – it reminds us of *facts*. Our security, as believers, rests not on theories, ideas or suppositions – but on facts. I have heard some theologians say that we can dispense with the facts of our faith and simply hang on to the teaching that arises from those facts. This is a subtle and dangerous suggestion and leads to great error. The exodus of the Israelites from Egypt was a fact. The giving of the law on Mount Sinai was a fact. The daily supply of manna in the wilderness (except on the Sabbath) was a fact. The crossing of the river Jordan was a fact. They are all great and glorious facts – facts of God. The death and resurrection of our Lord Jesus Christ is also a fact – something that belongs solidly to history.

When the future generations of Israel would ask: "What do these stones mean?", the reply would be given – something miraculous and wonderful happened here. When, today, the question is asked of us: "What do the bread and the wine on the Lord's Table mean?", the same answer must be given – something miraculous and wonderful happened here.

Christ, our Passover

Before looking in detail at the Passover which Jesus shared with His disciples, we must pause to deal with a relevant but controversial issue. I refer to the fact that, at first glance, there appears to be a contradiction in Scripture as to the actual date of that Passover. The difficulty can be seen when we compare two separate passages of Scripture, the first in Luke chapter 22 and the second in John chapter 18. The first reads: "And he said to them, 'I have eagerly desired to eat this Passover with you before I suffer'" (v.15). The second says: "Then the Jews led Jesus from Caiaphas to the palace of the Roman governor. By now it was early morning, and to avoid ceremonial uncleanness the Jews did not enter the palace; they wanted to be able to eat the Passover" (v.28).

The first passage mentions Jesus eating the Passover with His disciples, while the second indicates that the Passover was still to be celebrated, hence the Jews' refusal to go into the Roman governor's palace. Does this mean, as many have supposed, that what Jesus celebrated with His disciples was not the Passover but a simple family meal? No, for Jesus said quite clearly: "I have eagerly desired to eat *this* Passover with you."

Before we attempt to harmonise these two passages, it is important to keep in mind that there are no real contradictions in Scripture. Some passages of the Bible may look, at first glance, as if they are saying completely opposite things, but that is only because we may not have the deeper knowledge that reconciles two apparently contradictory passages. Rest assured, the inspired Scriptures can be relied on – no matter what the critics say.

There have been many attempts to explain the discrepancies between these passages, one view being that Jesus, anticipating the fact that He would die on the night the Passover would be celebrated (a Friday) decided to hold it one day earlier with His disciples. Another view says that as John's statement contradicts the three other gospel writers, he was obviously mistaken in what he wrote. Those who believe in the inspiration of Scripture find these explanations unacceptable.

The best explanation I have read is that offered by Joachim Jeremias in his book *The Eucharistic Words of Jesus*, in which he says that it was possible for the Passover to be eaten *officially* on two nights of the year. He claims that during this period of history the Pharisees and Sadducees were using calendars which differed from each other by a day. The Pharisees celebrated the Passover a day earlier, and, in the light of this, it was possible for Jesus to eat the Passover with those who followed the Pharisees (a Thursday) and go to the Cross on a Friday, at the time that the Sadducees were beginning their Passover celebrations.

If this was so, then it adds a rich and wondrous meaning to the words of Paul: "For Christ, our Passover lamb, has been sacrificed" (1 Corinthians 5:7). It would mean that Christ actually died on the Cross at the very time the ritualistic lambs were being slaughtered by the Sadducees at the temple in Jerusalem.

CHAPTER 3

FOCUS ON THE DISCIPLES

". . . he poured water into a basin and began to wash his disciples' feet." (John 13:5)

We focus our attention now on the interesting and dramatic events that went on in the Upper Room in Jerusalem, where Jesus observed the Passover feast with His disciples. Picture the scene with me. It is dusk, and Jesus and His disciples are reclining around a low table in an atmosphere that is pregnant with anticipation. Outside a storm is brewing that will eventually engulf the Son of God and sweep Him towards the cross. Our Lord had already seen the sun set for the last time. In less than eighteen hours, His limbs would be stretched, on what one writer calls "those grisly timbers of torture"; within twenty-four hours, He would be dead.

Evidently no servant was in attendance to wash the feet of those present – a usual courtesy of the day – so Jesus rises from the table, strips off His outer clothing, and, taking a towel and a bowl of water, proceeds to wash the disciples' feet (John 13:1–17). We said earlier that the disciples would face many surprises at this last crucial Passover. This was another – the Saviour who stooped to wash their feet.

Isn't it interesting that *none* of the disciples volunteered for that lowly task. They were so unsure of themselves that they dared not be humble – such an action might have caused them to lose their frail sense of identity. Jesus, on the other hand, had such a clear sense of identity – knowing that He had come from God and was going to God – that He could choose to be humble. How sad that the disciples were willing to argue over a throne (Mark 10:35–41), but not over a towel. Things haven't changed much in twenty centuries, have they?

True humility

"Jesus knew that the Father had put all things under his power, and that he had come from God and was returning to God; so he got up from the meal, took off his outer clothing, and wrapped a towel round his waist. After that, he poured water into a basin and began to wash his disciples' feet" (John 13:3–5). Notice how John, under the inspiration of the Holy Spirit, sees right into the mind of the Master before He stoops down to wash the disciples' feet. And what does he see? He sees our Lord's consciousness of His own greatness – He knew that He had come from God and was going to God. The consciousness of greatness is the secret of humility. Those who do not have a strong sense of their worth and value in God can never, in the true sense of the word, be humble. Their 'humility' borders more on self-belittlement. They do not *choose* to be humble for, more often than not, they are forced into situations about which they can do very little, except to say to themselves, "Well, now that I am here, I will be humble."

27

Humility is always a choice – a choice which arises out of a strong sense of one's worth and value. Notice this phrase: "Jesus knew that the Father had put all things under his power." Everything was under His control, in His hands! And what did He do with those hands? He used them to take a towel, pour water into a bowl and wash the disciples' feet. Knowing who He was made Him great – and humble. Great because humble and humble because great.

I can imagine that by the time Jesus got to Simon Peter, the arguing and small talk that had been going on between the disciples would have diminished. No doubt they began to realise how slow and insensitive they had been not to take the servant's role themselves. However, as Jesus bends before Peter, the disciple almost shouts: "No! Not my feet! You shall never wash my feet."

Is that what humility is – refusing to let Jesus wash one's feet? No, in fact, it sometimes takes more humility to be ministered to than it does to minister. You see, when we are always giving out to others, it is fairly easy to cover up our pride, but when we are put on the receiving end, and others are ministering to us, then our pride has nowhere to hide. Jesus said some strong words to Peter at this point: "Unless I wash you, you have no part with me" (John 13:8).

The firm rebuke penetrated Peter's defences, but rather than face his pride, he found another way out – the way of over-reaction: "Then, Lord, not just my feet, but my hands and my head as well!" (v.9).

After Jesus had brought about some balance in Peter's life, and had finished washing the disciples' feet, He sat back at the table and gave them this instruction: "Now that I, your Lord and Teacher, have washed your feet, you also should wash one another's feet" (v.14). Notice the words – "one another's feet". Had He said, "You ought to wash my feet," every disciple would have clamoured for the privilege. Who wouldn't stand in line to wash the Saviour's feet? But "one another's feet" – ah, that's different. That puts obedience to its maximum test.

Judas, the betrayer

We look now at another scene from the great drama that was enacted in the Upper Room on that first Maundy Thursday – our Lord's confrontation with Judas. It must have come as a great surprise to Judas when the Master made the announcement that there was someone present who was about to betray him. E.F. Kevan says: "It was the custom at the Passover feast for the presiding father, if there was an especially honoured guest, to break off a large piece of bread and give it to him first. It was that large piece that Jesus gave to Judas."

As soon as Judas received the bread from the hand of our Lord, we read that "Satan entered into him" (John 13:27). He then went out to put into action his plan of betrayal, and the Scripture cryptically says: "And it was night" (v.30). Night in Jerusalem, and night in his soul! How it must have hurt our Lord to be betrayed by one of His own disciples. In this hard and cruel world people expect to be shot at by their enemies, but no one, except a cynic, expects to be shot at by his friends.

Did you know that the origin of the superstition

concerning the number thirteen stems from this scene in the gospels? Thirteen sat down at the Last Supper, and one of them was a traitor. Superstitious people have dreaded the number thirteen ever since. Have you ever been betrayed? It's not easy to remain unembittered when someone who has stood at your side and claimed to be your friend lets you down. Jesus, despite the pain that the knowledge of Judas' betrayal caused Him, did not allow it to deter Him from ministering to the other disciples. Nor, too, must we.

Just who was Judas Iscariot and how do we explain his involvement in the betrayal of our Lord? It is believed by most Bible commentators that Judas was a Judean, and, if this was true, he would have been the only member of the apostolic band who was a southerner. Observe that, for it is not unimportant. Eleven of Christ's disciples were Galileans and only one came from the south. This would have meant that not only would Judas speak with a different accent, but his views and outlook on things would have been quite different from the rest of the group. This might have helped to ostracise him somewhat from the start. I am saying this not to excuse him but to explain him.

It seems also that he was a commercially-minded man, for our Lord appointed him to be the treasurer of the party – he had charge over the money (John 12:6). The little company, as it moved from place to place, needed someone to handle simple purchases, and, as Judas possessed some business acumen, he was the one chosen for the task. However, Judas was not only business-oriented, he was also a man with a covetous heart. We are told that he had been pilfering from the money bag a long time before he took the treacherous step of betraying our Lord.

With some natures, there is nothing so holy that money cannot besmirch. Watch money – it is so terribly useful and yet so terribly dangerous. The danger lying not in money of itself but in the way we regard it. How great is the temptation to become attached to it and yearn to possess it (1 Timothy 6:10). When money becomes our driving force, our god, then an enfeebled personality is the price we pay for the worship of that god.

Some Christian writers have expressed great sympathy for Judas. They feel that he had an unfair deal in life and has suffered from a bad press ever since. "After all," they say, "if Jesus had to die, somebody had to betray him. So why blame Judas? He was but the tool of providence, the victim of predestination."

The Bible certainly indicates that Jesus knew beforehand that He would be betrayed by Judas (John 6:64), but foreknowledge is not the same thing as foreordination. I know the sun will rise tomorrow but my knowing it does not make it rise. The foreknowledge that our Lord had concerning Judas did not compel him to act in the way he did – he was a free agent in it all. Judas got involved in the act of betrayal by following the same method that every one of us follows when we commit sin. First, we are tempted, then, instead of shunning the temptation or resisting it, we succumb to it, we entertain it. After that, it is just a downward spiral into sin.

However strong the Satanic influences were around Judas, there must have been a time when he opened himself to them. Jesus clearly regarded him as a responsible agent for, even at the last minute in the Upper Room, He carefully worded His statement so that Judas had an opportunity to recant. So dastardly was this action of Judas that, throughout history, whenever Maundy Thursday comes around, the first thing that occurs to us is this – it was the night on which our Saviour was betrayed.

CHAPTER 4

THE
FOUR
CUPS

". . . the cup of thanksgiving for which we give thanks . . ."
(1 Corinthians 10:16)

We turn now from looking at some of the personalities who were present in the Upper Room, when our Lord conducted the first Communion service, to focus on the Master Himself. How must Jesus have felt as He realised that He was setting up His own memorial service? What were the exact procedures that He went through as He celebrated this Passover of all Passovers? Where was the transition point when the Passover feast lost its significance and took on the nature of a new commemorative act? These are some of the questions we will come to grips with – but first we must acquaint ourselves with the way in which a Passover meal was conducted.

None of the four gospel writers give a detailed account of the exact procedures that were followed during a Passover meal – they focus more on the highlights of that memorable evening – so we have to depend on sources outside Scripture for information concerning this. I shall draw, therefore, on the writings of Jewish authors in order to describe the procedure of a Passover celebration during the time of Christ.

The cup of separation

Just after dusk on the night of the Passover, a Jewish family would gather round a table on which had been laid the various items described in chapter 2. The meal would begin with the father holding up the first of the four cups that were on the table and praying over it, after which all would then drink from it. This was called the "Cup of Kiddush", meaning separation or sanctification. It was the cup that separated this meal from all other meals, and marked it out as being different.

The four cups were reminders of the four promises of Exodus chapter 6 vv. 6–7: (1) "I will bring you out from under the yoke of the Egyptians"; (2) "I will free you from being slaves to them"; (3) "and will redeem you with an outstretched arm and with mighty acts of judgment"; (4) "I will take you as my own people, and I will be your God".

After the drinking of the first cup, the host would take a bowl of water and a towel and pass them around the table so that all could wash and dry their hands. He would then draw their attention to the bitter herbs and the bowl of salt water that were on the table, which they would be invited to taste – a reminder of the bitterness of slavery in Egypt and of the tears that had been shed so profusely by their forefathers.

The main course would then be brought out. This would consist of roast lamb, although it would not be eaten yet, thus reminding the family that it was through the shed blood of a lamb that their homes had been protected when the Angel of Death passed through Egypt. Also their attention would be drawn to the presence of the unleavened bread, indicating the need to leave behind them all reminders of Egyptian culture. After this would come the second eating of bitter herbs, a further reminder of the bitterness of bondage. A benediction was then offered in gratitude to God for His deliverance on that dark and fateful night.

The cup of explanation

After the second eating of the bitter herbs would come the drinking of the second cup which was called the "Cup of Hagadah" or the "Cup of Explanation". The father would once again lead the family in the drinking of this cup. At which point the youngest son in the family would be prompted to ask a series of formal questions, starting with: "Why is this night different from all other nights?" The head of the household would then give a potted history of Israel right down to the Passover meal, which heralded the deliverance from Egypt, explaining how this demonstrated God's everlasting power and mercy. Following this, the singing of the first part of what was called the Egyptian Hallel would begin. Hallel is the name given to the group of the psalms of praise (Psalms 113–118) which were used for Passover. Designated here were just Psalms 113 and 114.

Next came a second act of handwashing. The host would wash his hands and then prepare a 'sop' – a piece of unleavened bread filled with lamb and dipped in the paste called the 'charoseth'. He would give the first sop to the honoured guest on his left, then to the others sitting around the table. It was this 'sop' that our Lord offered to Judas, who was in the place of the honoured guest, and it was at this point during the Last Supper that Judas left to betray him. The roasted lamb would now be eaten, which, by tradition, had to be eaten entirely. Anything left over was to be destroyed and not used for a common meal.

The cups of blessing and praise

Once the lamb had been eaten, then came the drinking of the third cup, called the "Cup of Blessing". This cup was served with a piece of unleavened bread. When the cup had been drunk, the host would pronounce a blessing, a prayer of thanksgiving for the meal that they had eaten, after which would follow the singing of the rest of the Egyptian Hallel – Psalms 115 to 118. Then the fourth cup – the "Cup of Praise" – would be drunk, whereupon the family would sing what is known as "The Great Hallel" – Psalm 136. The singing of this would conclude the Passover meal.

We cannot be certain, of course, whether or not our Lord followed this precise procedure at the Passover feast, although I think we can safely assume that He did, apart from those moments when He gave the Passover a new direction. It is interesting to note that none of the gospel writers go into detail about the exact location of the room, the position of the disciples around our Lord, or the number of artefacts upon the table – all these things seemed to be considered as relatively unimportant. What was important, and every gospel writer recorded it, was the stunning revelation that Jesus gave concerning a new commemorative act that was to replace the ancient feast of the Passover. No wonder Jesus said, at the beginning of the meal: "I have eagerly desired to eat this Passover with you before I suffer." He longed to let them know that the story of His death had been hidden all the time within the Passover celebration – waiting to be revealed.

CHAPTER 5

FOCUS
ON
CHRIST

". . . Christ, our Passover lamb . . ." (1 Corinthians 5:7)

Now that we have familiarised ourselves with the traditional manner in which the feast of the Passover was conducted, we turn to consider what must have been going on in the heart and mind of the Master as He shared the Passover meal with His disciples. He was clearly aware of the fact that His death was imminent, as He had indicated when He said: "I have eagerly desired to eat this Passover with you *before I suffer.*"

The astonishing thing is that, even though our Lord knew that within twenty-four hours He would be dead and buried, it was clear He was thinking of His mission not as something that was past but as something that yet awaited Him. Normally, a person who has lived barely half the allotted span of life, when told he is about to die, would be plunged into deep depression. Kuebler Ross, the famous anthropologist, who has made a special study of the reactions people go through when they know they are about to die, says that there are five clear stages through which a person passes when confronted by the news that death is imminent.

I watched my wife go through these five stages when her doctors informed her that her sickness was terminal. However, I find nothing of this in the heart and mind of Jesus. He suffered intense grief in the Garden of Gethsemane but, as we shall see, this was not because He was unprepared or unwilling to die. The cross was not something our Lord ever tried to avoid: it was the reason why He came. He saw the cross not as the end of His mission but as the accomplishment of it – His lifelong goal.

Born to die

Have you seen that great painting by Holman Hunt entitled "The Shadow of Death"? It depicts the inside of the carpenter's shop in Nazareth and shows Jesus, stripped to the waist, standing by a wooden trestle on which He has put down His awl. He is obviously a little tired and stretches both His arms toward heaven. As He does so, the evening sunlight, flooding in through the open door of the little carpenter's shop, casts a dark shadow in the form of a cross on the wall behind Him. In the foreground can be seen His mother, Mary, who, kneeling among the chips of wood, looks up and is obviously startled as she sees her son's cross-like shadow on the wall.

Some regard this painting as sickly and sentimental, but the idea it contains is a Scriptural one – the cross loomed large in the mind and perspective of Jesus probably from His earliest days and certainly from the commencement of His ministry. Matthew chapter 16 v. 21 makes it quite clear that our Lord knew He was destined for a cross: "From that time on Jesus began to explain to his disciples that he must go to Jerusalem and suffer many things . . . that he must be killed and on the third day be raised to life". So horrified was He by Peter's insistence that He put the thought away from Him, that He addressed him with strange and uncharacteristically harsh words: "Out of my sight, Satan!" (Matthew 16:23). The vehemence was not aimed at Peter but at the Satanic ploy that was sounding through him. Nothing could deter Jesus from going to the cross – for He knew that this was the very reason why He had come.

The moment of revelation

We come now to the question which has intrigued Christians in every century: at what point in the evening did Jesus make clear to His disciples that He was replacing the annual celebration of the Passover by His own supper? We cannot be absolutely sure but most commentators believe it was probably after the drinking of the third cup – the "Cup of Blessing" – which, as we saw earlier, was accompanied by a prayer of thanksgiving.

There are two reasons for this belief – one is that Paul, in his first letter to the Corinthians (10:16), refers to the Communion cup as the cup of thanksgiving (NIV) or the cup of blessing (NKJ and NASB). The second is the fact that the cup of blessing was served with a piece of unleavened bread, at which time also the head of the household would say: "This is the bread of affliction which our fathers had to eat as they came out of Egypt." If this was the moment of revelation, then you can imagine how astonished the disciples must have been when Christ said those tremendous and powerful words: "This is my body given for you; do this in remembrance of me," and:

"This cup is the new covenant in my blood, which is poured out for you" (Luke 22:19–20).

This is the impact of what He was saying. Never again need you keep as the central focus of your worship the memory of your forefathers' deliverance from Egypt, for I am about to go to my death as the true Passover sacrifice. From now on, I want you to remember regularly an even greater event – the giving of my own body and blood for your redemption. In a few simple but powerful words, our Lord transformed an ancient ritual into the world's most wondrous revelation.

God's Paschal Lamb

A character in a play, standing in the wings with the lighting behind him, will cast a long shadow across the stage and, in this way, will attract the audience's attention. However, when the character himself steps on to the stage, whatever degree of interest the shadow aroused is surpassed by the wonder of seeing the character in person. This can be seen as an allegory of how, for long centuries, Jesus stood in the wings of history, casting His shadow before Him. He can be seen on almost every page of the Old Testament – in the deliverance of Israel from Egypt, in the sacrifices, in the details of the ancient tabernacle, in the ministry of the priesthood, and so on. Throughout the Prophetical books, predictions concerning the coming Messiah give the shadow more substance. Finally, four hundred years after the Old Testament was completed, John the Baptist made the declaration: "Look, the Lamb of God, who takes away the sin of the world!" (John 1:29).

Notice the words: "the Lamb of God who takes away the *sin of the world*". The Old Testament shows a progressive revelation as related to the offering of a lamb. First, a lamb (or ram) atoned for an individual, as in the case of Isaac (Genesis 22:13), then for a family, as in the first Passover and, finally, for a nation as on the Day of Atonement. The world waited for the day when a lamb would come whose sacrifice would take away not just the sins of an individual, a family, or even a nation, but the sins of the entire world. Now that day had arrived. And the sacrifice? None other than Jesus – God's Paschal Lamb.

"Do this in remembrance of me . . ."

When Jesus revealed Himself to His disciples as the Paschal Lamb, He gave them clear and definite instructions for His own memorial service. Reflect on the deep importance of what He was saying. His memorial was not to take place as a single occasion, like our modern-day memorial services – the final tribute of loved ones and friends – but it was to be a regular meal or service. He told them also that He desired this act of memorial to be repeated: "Do this in remembrance of me."

What were they to do? They were to follow His actions and use the words He Himself had used when He had broken the bread. I tend to feel that something is lacking in a Communion service when there is any departure from the act of taking, breaking, blessing, identifying and sharing the bread and the wine.

However, what do the bread and wine signify? The words Jesus spoke on that night make it crystal clear. Of the bread, He said: "This is my body which is given for you," and of the wine: "This cup is the new covenant in my blood, which is poured out for you." John Stott says of this moment: "The bread did not stand for His living body as He reclined with them at the table, but His body as it was shortly to be 'given' for them in death. Similarly, the wine did not stand for His blood as it flowed in His veins while He spoke to them, but His blood which was shortly to be poured out for them in death." It is clear from this that it is not so much by His life but by His death that Jesus wishes to be remembered. His life is important, but much more so is His death. Those who fail to recognise this, do so to their own spiritual peril.

Modern-day theologians who bypass the death of Christ and focus instead on such things as His exemplary life, His powerful words, His great miracles, and so on, have their priorities all wrong. The emphasis which Jesus places on His own death shows quite clearly that He regarded this as central to His purpose in coming to the world. Not that His exemplary life and character have no purpose – they most certainly have – but had He not died on the cross, then we would never have known what it means to be 'saved'.

One commentator puts it like this: "The Lord's Supper, which was instituted by Jesus, and which is the only regular commemorative act authorised by Him, dramatises neither His birth nor His life,

neither His words nor His works, but only His
death." What does this mean? It means this – it was
by His death that He wished, above all else, to be
remembered. You see, then, how essential the cross
is to Christianity. In a day and age when religionists
are attempting to turn the spotlight away from the
cross, and focus it instead on the life and words of
our Lord, we must do everything in our power to
proclaim the centrality of the cross. No cross – no
Christianity. It is as simple as that. I take my stand –
and I pray that you do too – with the hymnist who
said:

"Forbid it, Lord, that I should boast
Save in the death of Christ my Lord.
All the vain things that charm me most
I sacrifice them to His blood."

Making it personal

Before we leave the Upper Room and follow our Lord
into the Garden of Gethsemane, we draw one final
lesson from what went on in that memorable first
Communion service. It concerns the need for each
one of us to personally apply and appropriate the
death of Christ for ourselves. If, as we have been
saying, it was in the Upper Room that Jesus gave to
His disciples an advance dramatisation of His death
on the cross, it is important that we see further what
this was designed to convey.

The celebration of that first Communion did not
just involve Jesus, it involved all of the disciples.
Christ initiated it, but the others took part in it as

well. They could hardly have failed to get the message that it was not enough for the bread to be broken and the cup of wine to be handed to them – they had to eat and drink, and thus appropriate it for themselves. They were not spectators – they were participants.

What does all this say to us? It says that the death of Christ is the means by which we are saved; but we will not be saved until we receive and appropriate, for ourselves, the sacrifice He made for us on the Cross. This is extremely important for there are many who, when they are reminded of Christ's death on the cross, will think that, because of it, they are automatically forgiven. This is not so. Unless we get, as John Wesley said, the 'me' into the cross – Christ died for *me* – and personally receive His forgiveness by an appropriating act of faith, then the tragic situation is this – it will be as if He never died.

Prayer:

O Father, thank You for reminding me that it is only as I appropriate what Christ did for me on Calvary that I am saved. Even though I cannot fathom all the mystery of the cross, I can avail myself of its saving power. Thank You, Father. Amen.

CHAPTER 6

THE
FIRST
EASTER

"He is not here; he has risen, just as he said . . ." (Matthew 28:6)

Supper is now over and, after singing a hymn, Jesus and His disciples make their way down into the Kidron valley to a little olive orchard known as the Garden of Gethsemane. It was evidently a favourite retreat for Jesus. John comments that He had often met there with His disciples (John 18:2). Here something takes place which we have come to call "the agony in the Garden". It is obvious from the record that Christ is in great distress of soul, as, on three separate occasions, He prays a similar prayer: "My Father, if it is possible, may this cup be taken from me. Yet not as I will, but as you will" (Matthew 26:39).

What is this 'cup' which Jesus is talking about here? Is He recoiling from the physical suffering He is about to endure – the awful torture and agony of the cross? I cannot believe that it was purely this which brought Him such deep distress of soul. After all, had He not said: "Blessed are you when people insult you, persecute you . . . Rejoice and be glad" (Matthew 5:11–12)?

No – something much deeper than the thought of physical or even mental suffering was striking deep into His soul. The cup from which He shrank

symbolised neither the physical pain of being crucified, nor the mental distress of being humiliated and
despised, but rather the spiritual agony of bearing the
sins of the world. As Jesus looked into that cup and
saw the consequent spiritual separation from His
Father that would happen on the cross, His soul
recoiled in horror. No, it was not fear of death that
caused Him such agony, but the awful prospect of
being separated from the One to whom He had been
united throughout all eternity.

Each of the three prayers Jesus prayed began in
a similar way: "My Father, if it is possible . . ."
Although, in theory, everything is possible for God,
this was something that was God's purpose from the
very beginning – to save us from sin, and to save us
in a way that would satisfy His righteousness. This
would have been impossible without the substitu-
tionary death of the Saviour. No one else could have
borne our sins. There might be many who would be
willing to die for the sins of the world, but no one
who would be worthy to die. As the hymn so
beautifully puts it:

"There was no other good enough
    To pay the price of sin.
He only could unlock the gate
    Of heaven and let us in."

So, despite the begging and imploring nature of our
Lord's desperate prayer, it was a request which the
Almighty could not grant. However, God sent His
angelic messenger to strengthen and support Him
(Luke 22:43). I am so grateful – and so, I am sure, are

you – that on that dark night long ago, Jesus put that bitter cup to His lips and drained it dry.

Darkness at noon

Now we turn from gazing on our Lord's agony in the Garden to His agony on the cross. If the anticipation of bearing the wrath of God against sin was so terrible, then what must the reality have been like?

A strange and eerie darkness swept over Jerusalem on that awful day when Jesus was crucified, which seems to have lasted for three hours – from the sixth hour (noon) to the ninth hour (3 o'clock in the afternoon). What a contrast there was between our Saviour's birth and His death. As Douglas Webster puts it: "At the birth of the Son of God, there was brightness at midnight; at the death of the Son of God, there was darkness at noon."

What was the purpose of this strange phenomenon? I believe it was the outward symbol of the spiritual darkness that was enveloping our Lord as He "himself bore our sins in his body on the tree" (1 Peter 2:24). What is darkness in Biblical symbolism but separation from God, who is light and in whom there is no darkness at all (1 John 1:5)? The term 'outer darkness' is an expression that our Lord once used to describe hell, since it is absolute and utter exclusion from the light of God's presence. Grasp this thought firmly – at Calvary, our Lord, in some mysterious way, plunged into that 'outer darkness' and experienced, on our behalf, the awful terror of separation from God.

When Jesus emerged from the darkness that

enveloped Him, He uttered a strange and puzzling cry: "My God, my God, why have you forsaken me?" These words have come to be called by theologians and Bible students as the cry of dereliction. What is the explanation of these terrible words? Everyone agrees that Jesus was quoting from Psalm 22, but not everyone agrees as to the reason for this. Some say it was a cry of unbelief and despair – He was disappointed that His Father had not rescued Him from the awful horror of the cross. Others say it was a cry of loneliness – He was not really forsaken by God, but He *felt* forsaken. Another school of thought sees the words as a cry of victory for, as the psalm ends in a spirit of triumph and conquest, Jesus had this in mind when He spoke as He did.

I prefer to accept the words as they stand and believe them to be indicative of the fact that, due to the need for Christ to taste the full penalty of sin, an actual and dreadful separation, voluntarily accepted by both the Father and the Son, took place between them at the cross. Jesus not only felt forsaken – He was forsaken. It had to be if the Son was to fully taste the final consequence of human sin. And what was that final consequence? Separation from God. Jesus quoted this piece from Scripture as He had quoted other Scriptures, not because He was bewildered, stunned or confused but because He knew and believed He was fulfilling it.

He is alive!

On the third day after Christ had died upon the cross, He was miraculously brought back to life again, and it is this event which millions of Christians around the world joyfully celebrate on Easter day.

Historians tell us that at the Battle of Hastings in 1066, there was a moment when the Norman invaders were about to be overcome. For hours they had striven without success to storm Harold's stockades, and they were beginning to get weary and lose heart. A rumour began to spread among them which almost led to panic – a rumour which reported that their leader, William, had been slain. As soon as William heard it, he jumped on his horse and rode up and down the ranks shouting, "I am alive! I am alive! I am alive!"

What a graphic picture this is of our Lord on the first Easter day. Many of Christ's followers who were not present at the cross would have heard the sad news that He had been crucified and His body laid in a tomb. The report of His death would have been carried miles beyond the city of Jerusalem, and doubtless those who had believed in Him would have been deeply saddened and distressed. Our Lord, however, did not allow the news of His death to discourage His disciples for too long, as a little while later, He flung back from His face the mask of death and announced, first to Mary and then to other chosen disciples, "I am alive! I am alive! I am alive!"

It is important to understand exactly how Christ's death and resurrection are connected, for many Christians have a sentimental but not a very Scriptural understanding of these two momentous events. It is popularly believed that the resurrection is the way in which God turned the defeat of Good Friday into a glorious victory. However, that is not so. The death of Jesus on that first Good Friday was not a defeat but a victory, and the resurrection is that victory endorsed, demonstrated and proclaimed.

The apostle Peter, in his sermon on the Day of Pentecost, said: "It was impossible for death to keep its hold upon him" (Acts 2:24). It was possible for Him to die, but not possible for Him to be held by death. Why? Because on the cross, death had already been defeated. The evil principalities and powers, which had been conquered by His death on the cross, were at the moment of resurrection put under His feet and made subject to Him. "And God placed all things under his feet and appointed him to be head over everything . . ." (Ephesians 1:22).

Some Christians present Christ as a living Lord but place no emphasis on His atoning death, while others talk about His atoning death but fail to focus on His resurrection. The two events belong together and exclusion of one diminishes the other. Nothing would have been accomplished by Christ's death if He had not been raised from it, and nothing would have been accomplished by His resurrection if He had not dealt with death and defeated it on the cross. Good Friday was as much a victory as Easter Sunday.

Prayer:

My Father and my God, help me not to separate what You have joined together. Deepen my understanding of the cross and resurrection so that I might experience even more dynamically their power in my life. In Jesus' Name. Amen.

CHAPTER 7

THE
BREAKING
OF
BREAD

"They devoted themselves to the apostles' teaching and to the fellowship, to the breaking of bread and to prayer . . ." (Acts 2:42)

How faithfully, after the events of the cross and resurrection, did the disciples practise the Master's instructions concerning the regular celebration of Communion? Acts chapter 2 makes it clear that, within weeks of the Last Supper, the disciples had taught the converts the importance of this event, for we read: "They devoted themselves to the apostles' teaching and to the fellowship, to the *breaking of bread* and to prayer . . . Every day they continued to meet together in the temple courts. They *broke bread* in their homes and ate together with glad and sincere hearts . . ." (vv. 42 & 46).

It would appear from these verses that the actual practice of celebrating Communion was as part of a fellowship meal, but later the Church came to set aside a specific time in which they focused exclusively on remembering their Lord's sacrifice for them at Calvary: "On the first day of the week we came together to break bread" (Acts 20:7). By the time the first letter to the Corinthians was written (around AD 55), it is clear that the celebration of Communion was a regular practice in the Corinthian community, as evidenced by the phrase: "The cup of thanksgiving

for which we give thanks . . . the bread that we break"
(1 Corinthians 10:16).

What the Church of the first century practised
ought to be the practice of the Church now. I have no
hesitation in saying that to ignore the words of Jesus
– 'Do this' – is not just a slight omission, it is a sinful
omission. As we said earlier – if we do not do this in
remembrance of Him, it is doubtful whether we can
do anything in remembrance of Him.

There is only one passage in the epistles where the
purpose and meaning of Communion is expounded
and explained, that is in 1 Corinthians chapter 11. At
first it seems a little strange that the apostle Paul
should be writing about this, when we remember that
he was not present at our Lord's last meal with the
disciples. So, where did Paul get his deep understanding of Holy Communion? From one or more of the
original group of disciples? No – he got it directly
from the Lord himself: "For I received from the Lord
what I also passed on to you" (1 Corinthians 11:23).

Why was Paul chosen to be the one to give the only
exposition of the meaning of Communion? Why not
Simon Peter, or John? I believe that the reason for this
is because Paul had been given a special commission
to bring the gospel to the Gentiles (Romans 15:16). To
him also had been given the revelation of the true
nature of the Christian Church (Ephesians 3:1–11).
Two things emerge from this: one, that Paul was
specially gifted to make clear to the Gentiles the
significance of Old Testament truths that could easily
have eluded them; and two, the great apostle was
able, more than any of the other New Testament
writers, to expound the truths that related particularly

to the Church. As Holy Communion was intended by our Lord to be a corporate and not an individual celebration, something to be done within the context of the Body of Christ, then who better to instruct and apply that truth than the great apostle to the Gentiles?

Five clear aspects can be seen in the Lord's Supper, and keeping these in view, whenever we take Holy Communion, will, I believe, enable us to enter more fully into the meaning of this precious and sacred act. Firstly, the service of Communion is a corporate act in which the whole Christian community is expected to participate. Secondly, it is a commemorative act in which we focus on remembering our Lord's sacrificial and atoning death. Thirdly, it is a service in which the concept of covenant is highlighted. Fourthly, it is an act of celebration entered into with joy and thanksgiving. And fifthly, it is an act of commitment in which we dedicate ourselves more fully to representing our Lord Jesus Christ to a hostile, non-accepting world. These five aspects, when kept in mind as we come to the Communion table, will, I believe, help turn what can be a monotonous event into a momentous one. We owe it to God, and ourselves, to draw out from the Communion all that the Almighty has put into it.

True communion

The first thing we must understand about the Communion is that it is a corporate act. God never intended that we should partake of the Lord's Supper alone in the privacy of our own home. We must come together in order to celebrate it. In fact, we cannot Scripturally observe the Lord's Supper unless we come together. Sometimes Christians use the word 'communion' to describe their times of private prayer and fellowship with the Lord, but the word 'communion', when applied to the Lord's Supper, means more than that – it means fellowship with other Christians also. If you want an interesting evening reading your Bible, go through the Acts of the Apostles and observe the number of times the word 'together' or its synonyms occur. You will come to the conclusion that the early Church was a very 'together' fellowship.

The celebration of Holy Communion, then, highlights the fact that the church is not simply a group of individuals but a community. Notice Paul's words: "Is not the cup of thanksgiving for which we give thanks a participation in the blood of Christ? And is not the bread that we break a participation in the body of Christ?" (1 Corinthians 10:16). At the Communion table, we not only share in Christ but we share in each other. Everyone who belongs to Christ belongs to everyone else who belongs to Christ. There is no such thing as a solitary Christian.

Paul's exposition of the Communion in 1 Corinthians chapter 11 begins with a strong rebuke which he felt obliged to give to the church because of certain irregularities that were allowed to creep in amongst them. Apparently, in the church at Corinth, the act of remembering the Lord's death was preceded by a 'love feast' – a communal meal to which all would contribute. Somehow the meal had become degraded into a free-for-all act. There were divisions – the rich would sit on one side and enjoy their sumptuous provisions, while the poor would find a separate place to eat their meagre fare. Then, immediately after the eating of this meal, came the celebration of the Lord's Supper.

Paul was concerned because the evident lack of love that was demonstrated at the so-called 'love feast' spilled over into the act of Communion, and thus the two contradicted each other. What should have been an act of communion was really nothing more than an act of collaboration. They sat together, but their hearts did not belong to one another. They came together physically, but they did not come together spiritually.

The problem that existed in the Corinthian church is with us today. Believers meet together to celebrate the Lord's Supper, but never experience true communion. Thus, sadly, it cannot be said of them, as it was said of the church after Pentecost: "All the believers were one in heart and mind" (Acts 4:32).

Koinonia

The best word to describe the deep spiritual fellowship which Christ looks for between believers is the Greek word *koinonia* – literally 'fellowship'. This fellowship, however, goes deeper than mere camaraderie or friendliness. In the words of George Fox: "The church experiences a relationship where they seek to know each other in that which is eternal." Other relationships let us know each other in that which is temporal or transient; the relationship we have with one another in Christ, however, transcends the temporal. We get to know each other "in that which is eternal".

Without this deep fellowship, the church is no better than a fraternity or a club. One of the reasons why the Christians in the early Church turned the world upside down was because they had a clear understanding of their relationship with God and their relationship with one another. They had a true sense of community.

Where and how can this *koinonia*, this deep sense of fellowship and community, be cultivated and developed. One place is at the Lord's Table. The regular celebration of Holy Communion greatly assists in heightening our sense of community. All gathering together, of course, contributes to a sense of community, but the Lord's Table plays a special part in producing that deep, inner fellowship.

As we gather round the table on which the bread and wine are placed, we are reminded not only of our oneness in Christ, but the thought is borne in upon us that we are a community of the cross. The regular exposure of our minds and spirits to the sight of the emblems, which our Lord chose to perpetuate the memory of His death, vividly brings home to us that, having been brought into being by the cross, we must continue to live by and under the cross. All our perspectives and behaviour must be governed by the cross.

Just as the cross enables us to enjoy and experience a new relationship with God, so it enables us to enjoy and experience a new relationship with one another. If there is one place where we need to open our lives to the power of the cross, it is in the area of relationships. "Christianity," says Dr E. Stanley Jones, "is the science of living well together with others according to Jesus Christ."

Many of our attempts to live together in harmony are haphazard; they do not obey the principles that flow from the cross. In fact, the way some Christians relate to each other is a denial of all that the cross and the Lord's Table represent. The bread and wine portray and symbolise not just our togetherness in Christ but that our lives must be governed and regulated by the principles of the cross.

A community of the cross

Some prefer to think of themselves as the community of the resurrection rather than the community of the cross, and, although the former is true, it must be recognised that the table our Lord perpetuated has upon it not the symbols of the resurrection but the symbols of the cross. The resurrection is very much part of it – a glorious and integral part – but the main focus is on the cross.

Are our relationships with one another governed and regulated by the cross? When we eat and drink together at the Lord's Table are we just together physically but poles apart spiritually? Each Christian has within them the potential for giving joy or pain in their relationships. When we relate well together, the result is joy; if we relate badly, the result is pain. It is at the point of pain, however, that a cross becomes inevitable. For what is a cross? It is the point at which love crimsons into suffering. Jesus loved us so much that He was willing to suffer for us. In a similar way that is what we must do for each other, for Calvary love is suffering, self-sacrificing love. It holds on to relationships, no matter how difficult they may be. It is prepared to suffer, when necessary, the pain that sometimes is inevitable when disputes arise. It holds no prejudices against people of a different culture and race. It is willing to be misunderstood without augmenting misunderstandings. Disagreements do not make it disagreeable.

CHAPTER 8

THE
LORD'S
COMMAND

". . . 'This is my body given for you; do this in remembrance of me.'" (Luke 22:19)

We move on now to examine the second aspect of Communion – commemoration. We are commanded to come together in order to remember Him. Our Lord does not just invite us to His Table but insists on us being there. Does this sound too harsh and demanding? Surely, though, when our Lord insists on something, there is a wise and loving purpose behind it. His demands are not the demands of an autocrat who delights in having his own way – they are the demands of one who has our highest interests at heart. If this seems difficult to grasp, then remember: the one who commands you is the one who was crucified for you. Consider His words once again: "Do this in remembrance of me." Not: "I *suggest* you do this," or "*Try* and do this." It is quite clearly a command.

Some believe that this command was intended to apply only to the original group of disciples, and not to the continuing life of the Church. However, there are two strong arguments that can be brought against this view. Firstly, the word 'do', in the original Greek, suggests repetition. Secondly, the words, "I received from the Lord what I also passed on to you" (1 Corinthians 11:23) show it to be an authoritative command from the Lord for the whole church. In the light of this, can there be any doubt that it is a divine command, not to be ignored?

Whenever I read the words: "Do this in remembrance of me," my first thought is how sad that we, who are redeemed, should need a reminder at all. One would think that once we come to Christ and understand just what His death has procured for us, it would remain in our consciousness every moment of the day. However, as we know, such is not the case. We are very apt to forget. I heard of one man who referred to his memory as the thing he forgot with! Another spoke bitterly of it as 'that traitor'. Someone else, who was lent the same book on several different occasions, not realising that he had read it before, said: "An excellent book, but the author tends to repeat himself." My mother would never admit that she had a poor memory, instead referring to it as "a good forgettory".

To help guard against our natural forgetfulness, therefore, Christ instituted the sacrament. He knew how the simple ordinance would help quicken our memory. We look at the bread and wine, and the sight of them triggers our memory, helping to bring Calvary more clearly to mind. So, our frequent failure to focus on our Lord's death, and its meaning for our lives, has its finest antidote here – regular attendance at the Lord's Table. The feast banishes forgetfulness. We remember, because we are reminded.

Why do we forget?

Another reason why we can so easily forget our Lord, and what He has done for us on the cross, is because we have never seen Him. Although He has been depicted in paintings and sculptures, the gospels do not give us as much as a hint regarding His physical appearance. We can identify with Egbert Sandford's words from his poem "An Easter Wish":

"I know that He lived here, for I can trace
   Rare marks of His manhood in every place,
But I wish I had met Him face to face."

Ian Macpherson aptly puts it: "What we see seems real and what we cannot see, unreal. The visible impinges vividly upon our consciousness; the invisible inclines to recede into oblivion." The invisibility of Christ, therefore, is one reason why we can easily overlook His reality and forget what He has done for us – yet this need not be so. The Communion table with its simple emblems stimulates the memory: the bread is graphically reminiscent of His flesh; the wine, of His blood. To the devout and reverent imagination, the precious and sacred emblems give substance to the reality of the unseen Redeemer, and so we recall His atoning death and sacrifice for us.

Yet another reason why we can so easily forget our Lord's redemptive sacrifice for us on the cross is the constant pressure of the world around us. As Wordsworth put it: "The world is too much with us." The population of the earth, so I am told, is somewhere in excess of four billion. However, as someone put it: "There is always One more who is never taken account of in any census – the living Christ Himself."

The people who mill around us every day of our lives have a great influence upon us. Their words, their laughter, their tears, their anger, their gestures, their blasphemies all affect us, albeit subconsciously. However, we can still see, hear and touch them, but the One whom no census recognises is intangible and inaudible. It is natural, therefore, that the people with whom we rub shoulders day by day tend to influence us more than the spiritual realities which we know exist but cannot see or hear.

Our Lord anticipated this problem when He instituted the Communion service – this wondrous "feast of memory". Knowing how the world would impinge upon us and how influential it would be, He ordained that, in the life of the church, there should be regular seasons of remembrance, when, with the graphic symbols of His presence before us, we deliberately and purposefully call Him to mind. I have been amazed at how powerfully our Lord can make Himself known in the breaking of the bread.

Notice, however, that our Lord does not ask us to remember the date, or the place, but *Him*. He does not say: "Do this in remembrance of my death"; although, of course, the fact that He died a redemptive death can never be far from our minds as we eat the bread and drink the cup. I think that what our Lord had in mind when He uttered these words can be paraphrased like this: "Do this in remembrance of all that I am to you." It is vitally important that we grasp what our Lord intended here, for there are some who focus more on the fact than the person. Remember, it is not 'this', 'that' or the 'other' that saves us – it is Christ who saves us.

When Dr Charles Edwards of Bala, the great Welsh theologian, was busy working on his book about the Atonement, a thought burst in upon him that seemed to set his soul on fire. Jumping from the desk at which he was sitting, he dashed out into the street shouting excitedly: "Jesus *is* the Atonement! Jesus *is* the Atonement." Then, going back to his study, he wrote: "This is the Atonement, not the sufferings and not the death, but the person of the Son of God in the sufferings and death." This must always be the central focus of our minds whenever we approach the Communion table – not just the time, the date, the action, or the place – but *Him*.

CHAPTER 9

A
NEW
COVENANT

". . , Jesus the mediator of a new covenant . . ." (Hebrews 12:24)

We come now to the third aspect of the Communion – the aspect of covenant. I have met many Christians over the years who are turned off by the word 'covenant'. They feel that it is a word which describes the technicalities of the faith – something to be debated in theological seminaries rather than discussed at an ordinary level.

There are two things about this that I would like to point out. Firstly, the concept underlying the Biblical word 'covenant' is something even the youngest Christian can grasp. Secondly, not to grasp it means you will miss out on the real meaning that lies behind the Communion. No one can truly comprehend Holy Communion unless they understand its covenant character.

In all the four records given of the institution of the Lord's Supper, we find an allusion to covenant. "This is my blood of the new covenant" (Matthew 26:28). Mark uses identical words and Luke, similar ones. Paul writes: "This cup is the new covenant in my blood" (1 Corinthians 11:25). Notice particularly the words in Matthew's account: "This is my blood . . . which is poured out for many for the *forgiveness of sins.*" Just imagine the tremendous truth that lies within these words – through the shedding of the Saviour's blood, God was taking the initiative to establish a new pact or covenant with His people, out of which would come the blessing of forgiveness for sin. God, of course, has always been *willing* to forgive sin, but, because of its heinous and serious nature, some kind of 'satisfaction' was necessary. The Old Testament sacrifices were not sufficient – a new way had to be found. At the Last Supper, Jesus broke the news that a new way had been found. Hallelujah!

Sealed by blood

What exactly is a covenant? The dictionary meaning of the word signifies a mutual undertaking or agreement between two or more parties, each binding the other to its full obligations. The Biblical word for covenant (Greek: *diatheke*), however, does not in itself contain the idea of joint obligation; it usually signifies a promise or an undertaking given by a single person. To understand the idea behind the covenant about which Jesus spoke at the Last Supper, we must take a brief look at Jewish history.

Many centuries before Jesus came, God had entered into a covenant with Abraham, sealed by blood, in which He promised to bless him and bring him into a good and prosperous land (Genesis chapter 15). Later, God renewed that covenant with Abraham's descendants – the Israelites – after He had rescued them from slavery in Egypt (Exodus chapter 24). Hundreds of years after this, in the seventh century BC, when the people had forsaken God and broken His covenant many times, the

Almighty gave Jeremiah this promise: "The time is coming . . . when I will make a new covenant with the house of Israel and with the house of Judah" (Jeremiah 31:31). However, when the first covenant to Abraham was inaugurated, it was sealed by blood, and such was the case when the covenant was renewed at Sinai; but there is no mention of blood in the covenant to Jeremiah. It is like a legal document drawn up but not signed or witnessed. When and how will it be made valid? Well, we have to pass on a further six centuries before we learn how that covenant was ratified.

After years of patient waiting, and increasing expectancy, Jesus, the Son of God, stood in an upper room in Jerusalem and announced that the blood of God's new covenant would be none other than His own. What a breathtaking moment that must have been. Picture the scene once again. Our Lord takes up the bread, which was normally used at this stage in the Passover meal, and dedicates it to a new purpose. The ancient Passover, celebrated in the same way for centuries, is now being given a new direction. "In the same way, after the supper he took the cup, saying, 'This cup is the new covenant in my blood, which is poured out for you'" (Luke 22:20).

It was at this point that the Passover was transformed – it became the Lord's Supper of the new covenant. Jesus was saying, in effect: "The new covenant, promised by Jeremiah, has been waiting for centuries to be ratified and sealed. Now that hour has come, and the blood that seals it is the blood that flows out of my own veins. This cup is the symbol of that. Drink it in remembrance of me." So every time you approach the Communion table, let your mind dwell on the thrilling thought that our Lord died to bring us into a new covenant relationship with God.

A covenant of grace

The old covenant, made with Abraham, is often referred to as the covenant of law, and the new covenant, announced through Jeremiah and sealed with Christ's blood, is known as the covenant of grace. The difference between them is this: the Law says, in effect, "Do this and you shall live." Grace says: "I will do it for you." This is why the new covenant is superior to the old. As Paul wrote: "Christ redeemed us from the curse of the law by becoming a curse for us, for it is written: 'Cursed is everyone who is hanged on a tree.' He redeemed us in order that the blessing given to Abraham might come to the Gentiles through Christ Jesus, so that by faith we might receive the promise of the Spirit" (Galatians 3:13 & 14). The Law was imposed from without, but Christ lives within us by His Spirit, enabling us to live lives that please and honour Him.

As mentioned earlier, a covenant normally involves two or more parties, and the principle underlying it is: if you will do your part, I will do mine. However, the word *diatheke* suggests that it is a covenant ordained and laid down by an authority. It is not God and man making an equal contribution, but God taking on the full obligation. There is a human side to it, of course, but compared to God's input, it is minimal. There need be no fear that because of human weakness and frailty it will break down. As one preacher quaintly put it: "God thought it, Christ bought it, the Holy Spirit wrought it and, though the devil fought it, thank God, I've got it." Got it, for ever!

We have already touched on the fact that one of the exciting features of the new covenant was that it promised the forgiveness of sins, but let us now look at this aspect more closely. Under the old covenant, sin could not be dealt with effectively: "because it is impossible for the blood of bulls and goats to take away sins" (Hebrews 10:4). The Old Testament sacrifices served as a type or precursor for the New. God did not previously overlook sin, but rather 'looked over' it to the coming perfect sacrifice of His Son on Calvary.

I hope you are not one to object to the use of the word 'blood' in books or hymns about the Christian faith. "The blood of Christ" is one of the most sacred and significant phrases in the whole of Scripture. Those who say that it is crude and savours of paganism need to revise their thinking. Blood flows everywhere in the Bible. The red 'thread', so to speak, runs from Genesis to Revelation. "In fact, the law requires that nearly everything be cleansed with blood, and without the shedding of blood there is no forgiveness" (Hebrews 9:22). It is not just by the death of Christ that we are saved, it is through death *by the shedding of blood*. His blood is covenant blood. It is not merely blood poured out in affectionate self-giving. It is the blood of a covenant sacrifice in which God commits Himself to us in the most solemn way possible. Edward More puts it beautifully in his hymn:

"His oath, His covenant and blood,
  Support me in the 'whelming flood;
When all around my soul gives way,
  He then is all my hope and stay."

CHAPTER 10

THANKSGIVING

"Let us come before him with thanksgiving . . ." (Psalm 95:2)

We come now to look at the fourth aspect of Communion – the aspect of celebration. One of the words used to describe the Lord's Supper is the word *Eucharist*, which simply means *thanksgiving*.

The Communion service ought to be a time when we open our hearts to God in joyful celebration and praise as we remind ourselves of the nature of the new covenant. It is not just meant to be a time when we remind ourselves that we are a corporate body, meeting together to commemorate the death of our Lord, it is a time to give thanks as our Lord did prior to distributing the bread and wine at the Last Supper: "And when he had given thanks . . ." (1 Corinthians 11:24). Following the conclusion of the Passover meal, we read that our Lord and His disciples sang a hymn (Matthew 26:30). A Communion service, so I believe, though focusing on very solemn and profound truths, ought not to be doleful.

I could never understand why the Communion services I attended in the early days of my Christian experience seemed so gloomy and sorrowful until I questioned those who took part. It seems they felt that the sufferings of Christ on the cross ought to be responded to with sympathy and sorrow. Although I believed that to be true, and still do, I used to say to them, "Yes, we must start there but we must not stop there. After we remember His suffering and sacrifice for us, our hearts should respond in grateful worship and praise." After nearly forty years as a Christian, I have seen no reason to change my view. So I say with increased conviction – at the Communion table, we must not only remind ourselves of our Lord's redemptive sacrifice, we must *rejoice* in it, too.

A time to celebrate

E.F. Kevan points out that the Lord's Supper is a meal and, throughout time, "meals have been the occasions of conviviality and of friendship." He goes on to say, "A feast is the method for expressing joy. When you have a birthday, you have a birthday party; when you get married, you have a wedding breakfast. When we want to express our gladness in any matter, we have a common meal together, and this is one of the aspects that the Lord has taken up in His ordinance of the Lord's Supper."

As we have not yet developed the thought that the Lord's Supper is a spiritual feast, this seems to be an appropriate moment to do so. "I am the bread of life. He who comes to me will never go hungry, and he who believes in me will never be thirsty" (John 6:35). Although these words of Jesus do not have a direct reference to the Communion, they are, nevertheless, a description of what happens when we meet together at the Lord's Table. We *feed* on Him. Just as we *eat* the bread, not merely look at it, and just as we *drink* the wine, not merely observe it, so, in the

Communion, we partake of Christ and feed our souls upon Him. One critic of the gospels has described the verse which says: "Unless you eat the flesh of the Son of Man and drink his blood, you have no life in you" (John 6:53) as "Christian cannibalism". He evidently did not understand how the soul can draw strength and nourishment from regular contact with Christ. It is a mystery but do not let the mystery of it hinder you from experiencing it and enjoying it. I say *enjoying* for one can no more partake of Christ without enjoying Him than one can partake of a good meal and not experience a degree of pleasure.

Continuous celebration

In 1 Corinthians chapter 5 vv. 7–8, Paul expresses the mutual sense of joy and exhilaration that we experience in Christ by alluding to the most well-known of all the Jewish feasts – the feast of Passover. "For Christ, our Passover lamb, has been sacrificed. Therefore let us keep the festival . . ."

We have said so much about the Passover already that there seems little else left to say, but actually there is. Although, strictly speaking, the Passover was the communal meal eaten during the evening of what the Jews call "the fifteenth Nisan", it came to be applied also to the week-long feast of Unleavened Bread which followed. Both the Passover meal itself and the week that followed was, and is to this day, a time of great rejoicing for the nation of Israel. The basis of that rejoicing was their deliverance from the tyranny and bondage of Egypt. However, a greater exodus than that enjoyed by Israel has been effected in human history: the deliverance made possible by Jesus Christ on the cross of Calvary. Because He, the Paschal Lamb, has been slain and, by His blood, we have been set free, we are exhorted to keep the feast.

However, what does Paul mean by: "Therefore let us keep the festival"? Is he saying that we ought to keep the ancient feast of the Passover just as the Jews do to this day? No, I believe he is saying that the whole of the Christian life should be thought of as a festival in which we continuously celebrate what God has done for us in Christ. Although, in this sense, the Christian life is a continuous festival, the Lord's Supper – the particular Christian equivalent to the Passover – is a powerful means of crystallising the truth, and bringing home to us the need and reason for continuous celebration.

In this way, the Communion service, or Eucharist, helps us keep in focus the purpose that lies behind our rejoicing, namely, the sacrificial death of our Lord Jesus Christ, God's Paschal Lamb. Just as the Passover was central to Israel's life and identity, so the Lord's Supper is central to the church's life.

There are many reasons that lie behind the praise of God's people when they meet together in church, but the central reason must always be gratitude for our deliverance from the bondage of sin, accomplished through our Saviour's atoning death on the cross. When we focus on the cross, we are caught up in the worship of heaven, and join with the angels and archangels to acknowledge the worth of our Creator and our Redeemer. "In a loud voice they sang: 'Worthy is the Lamb, who was slain, to receive power and wealth and wisdom and strength and honour and glory and praise!'" (Revelation 5:12). To focus on the cross and not want to burst out in praise means that we do not fully realise what it is all about.

W.M. Clow points out that: "A Buddhist temple never resounds with a cry of praise nor do Mohammedan worshippers ever sing. Their prayers are, at the highest, prayers of submission and request. They seldom reach the gladder note of thanksgiving and are never jubilant with the songs of the forgiven." How different the atmosphere can be in a Christian church. The rafters may ring with praise. And why not? If angels sing of the cross (Rev. 5:11–12) who have never tasted its power, then how much more we who are sinners saved by grace?

CHAPTER 11

A
CALL
TO
COMMITMENT

". . . you cannot have a part in both the Lord's table and the table of demons" (1 Corinthians 10:21)

We come now to the last of our five aspects of the Communion – commitment. In ancient times, and, indeed, in some parts of the world today, eating a meal at someone's table implied a certain degree of commitment. You may have heard the phrase, "the salt of the covenant". This arose from eating salt with someone, or, in other words, enjoying a meal with them. It was expected of those who ate at another's table that they would never do anything to violate the friendship that had been shown them.

This kind of 'table fellowship' is referred to in the book of Obadiah: "Those who eat your bread will set a trap for you" (v. 7). Here we see that the sacred loyalties which had been worked out together were being violated. Psalm 41 also illustrates this: "Even my close friend, whom I trusted, he who shared my bread, has lifted up his heel against me" (v. 9). The thing that troubled the psalmist was not so much that he had been wronged but that he had been wronged by someone who had sat at his own table. It was this verse Jesus quoted (John 13:18) with reference to Judas.

It is clear, therefore, from Scripture that taking a meal with someone implies a trust and a pledge. In a way, this is how we should view the taking of Communion. Our Lord expects that when we eat and drink at His table, we will not be a party to anything that would injure His cause or violate His eternal principles. Dare we eat and drink with Him and then go out and bring dishonour to His name?

All that we have just considered takes on a deeper significance when we remember God's warnings to His people not to partake in heathen feasts: "Be careful not to make a treaty with those who live in the land; for when they prostitute themselves to their gods and sacrifice to them, they will invite you and you will eat their sacrifices" (Exodus 34:15); "While Israel was staying in Shittim, the men began to indulge in sexual immorality with Moabite women, who invited them to the sacrifices to their gods. The people ate and bowed down before these gods . . . And the Lord's anger burned against them" (Numbers 25:1–3).

Paul takes up this point vividly when he writes to the Corinthians: "Consider the people of Israel: Do not those who eat the sacrifices participate in the altar? . . . the sacrifices of pagans are offered to demons, not to God, and I do not want you to be participants with demons. You cannot drink the cup of the Lord and the cup of demons too; you cannot have a part in both the Lord's table and the table of demons" (1 Corinthians 10:18–21). The clear meaning of all this is that the table at which we eat is, whether we realise it or not, the place where our loyalty is pledged.

Spiritual health

This is why we should always approach the Lord's table with a willingness to scrutinise our habits, our motives, and our lifestyle, and be prepared to break with all those things that dishonour Him. This self-examination is healthy and for our own good, as Paul writes: "A man ought to examine himself before he eats of the bread and drinks of the cup. For anyone who eats and drinks without recognising the body of the Lord eats and drinks judgment on himself" (1 Corinthians 11:28 & 29). To strike this solemn note is necessary, and one which we cannot and dare not avoid. If we fail to examine ourselves when we come to the Communion table, and surrender to the Lord those things that are wrong, then they will become the disease germs within us that will bring about our spiritual ill-health. How important, however, it is to permanently keep firmly in mind that the purpose of self-examination is not to berate ourselves with how terrible we are, but to surrender our failures to Christ, receive His forgiveness and move a little closer towards Him.

In his letter, Paul also warned: "Therefore, whoever eats the bread or drinks the cup of the Lord in an unworthy manner will be guilty of sinning against the body and blood of the Lord" (1 Corinthians 11:27). What did he mean? Eating and drinking in an unworthy manner means participating in the Communion in a factious and judgmental spirit. This is a sin not just against the Body of Christ, the Church, but against the Person of Christ as symbolised in the elements.

Almost every local church has those among its members who come to the Lord's Table bent on examination – not of themselves, but of others. I have no hesitation in saying that this attitude produces spiritual ill-health and decay. Paul makes it quite clear: "That is why many among you are weak and sick, and a number of you have fallen asleep" (1 Corinthians 11:30). There were those in the Corinthian church who failed to examine themselves at the Lord's Table. They maintained their wrong behaviour and attitudes, and became weak and sickly as a result, some even died. So, you see, spiritual ill-health can turn to physical ill-health. Dare I say it? There are some in the Christian Church today who are sicker than they should be. However, if we approach the Lord's Table in the right spirit, then we will be able to approach the whole of life in the right spirit.

CONCLUSION

UNTIL
HE
COMES

"For whenever you eat this bread and drink this cup, you proclaim the Lord's death until he comes." (1 Corinthians 11:26)

As we finish this study, we remind ourselves of the five 'C's of Communion – community, commemoration, covenant, celebration and commitment. Most Christians, irrespective of denomination, will agree that whenever we approach the Lord's Table, we must recognise that it is a corporate act in which we focus our attention on Christ's redemptive death on Calvary, remind ourselves of its covenant nature, rejoice in the great benefits of the atonement, and pledge our loyalty to Him who loved us and gave Himself for us.

There is just one more point I want to add – the Lord's Supper is a wonderful but only a temporary provision for the Christian Church. We shall not celebrate it in eternity for there, faith will be lost in sight – we do it only "until He comes". "For whenever you eat this bread and drink this cup, you proclaim the Lord's death until he comes" (1 Corinthians 11:26).

As we move away from the Communion table, we must bear in mind the thrilling thought that just as Christ came at the first advent so will He come again at the second advent. The Lord's Supper demands, therefore, a confident belief in our Lord's second coming; it is the token of our Master's return. Indeed, without that belief, it cannot be said to be truly celebrated. So remember: The Lord's Supper is to be celebrated "until He comes".

George Rawson's compelling rhyme puts it very powerfully:

"And thus that dark betrayal night
　With the last advent we unite
By one blest chain of loving rite
　Until He come."

Prayer:

O Father, what can I say? My heart cries out in eager anticipation: "Even so, come, Lord Jesus." Amen.

Also in The Understanding Series

UNDERSTANDING GUIDANCE
Selwyn Hughes

In *Understanding Guidance*, Selwyn Hughes discusses the problems and perplexities we all face as Christians who are trying to lead a God-guided life.

Finding God's will, he shows, is not about following formulas; it is maintaining a loving relationship with the One who wants to guide us. Upon this foundation, he takes a careful look at the ways God guides and the freedom He gives for us to choose.

A final section offers a practical step by step guide to knowing God's will.

UNDERSTANDING THE PRESENCE OF GOD
Selwyn Hughes

Christians have the assurance that they are constantly surrounded by the presence of God, for He has said "I will never leave you nor forsake you" (Heb. 13:5, NKJ). Honesty compels us to admit, however, that we do not always feel it.

Selwyn Hughes asks the question, "What can we do to increase, enhance and understand better the sense of God's presence?" His answer reveals how we can co-operate with the Holy Spirit, who longs to increase our awareness of His presence with us.